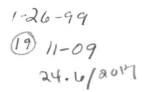

Animal Survival

HOW ANIMALS PROTECT THEMSELVES

Michel Barré

Gareth Stevens Publishing
MILWAUKEE

For a free color catalog describing Gareth Stevens' list of high-quality books and multimedia programs, call 1-800-542-2595 (USA) or 1-800-461-9120 (Canada). Gareth Stevens Publishing's Fax: (414) 225-0377.
See our catalog, too, on the World Wide Web: http://gsinc.com

The editor would like to extend special thanks to Jan W. Rafert, Curator of Primates and Small Mammals, Milwaukee County Zoo, Milwaukee, Wisconsin, for his kind and professional help with the information in this book.

Library of Congress Cataloging-in-Publication Data

Barré, Michel, 1928-
    [Comment s'abritent les animaux. English]
    How animals protect themselves / by Michel Barré.
        p. cm. — (Animal survival)
    Includes bibliographical references (p. 47) and index.
    Summary: Discusses some of the different ways animals provide shelter
for themselves and protect themselves from predators, from birds' nests
and beehives to camouflage and porcupine quills.
    ISBN 0-8368-2080-0 (lib. bdg.)
    1. Animals—Habitations—Juvenile literature. 2. Animal defenses—
Juvenile literature. [1. Animals—Habitations. 2. Animal defenses.]
I. Title. II. Series: Barré, Michel, 1928- Animal survival.
QL756.B35513 1998
591.47—dc21   97-40156

This North American edition first published in 1998 by
Gareth Stevens Publishing
1555 North RiverCenter Drive, Suite 201
Milwaukee, Wisconsin 53212 USA

This U.S. edition © 1998 by Gareth Stevens, Inc. Original © 1993 by Éditions MANGO-Éditions PEMF, under the French title *Comment s'abritent les animaux?*. Additional end matter © 1998 by Gareth Stevens, Inc.

Translated from the French by Janet Neis.
U.S. editor: Rita Reitci
Editorial assistant: Diane Laska

Series consultant: Michel Tranier, zoologist at the French National Museum of Natural History

The editors wish to thank the Jacana Agency and the artists who kindly granted us permission to use the photographs displayed in the following pages:

Cover, J. P. Varin, W. Layer; 4, J. P. Varin; 5, R. Volot; 6, F. Winner; 7, F. Danridal, M. Moisnard; 9, C. de Klein, Rouxaine; 10, P. Summ, E. Lemoine, Ramade; 13, Frédéric, G. Renson, T. McHugh; 14, Hellio-Van Ingen; 15, F. Winner, Y. Gladu; 17, A. Ducros, Rouxaine, R. Dulhoste; 18, F, Winner; 19, Henrion; 20, R. König; 21, K. Ross, J. P. Varin; 22, J. P. Champroux; 23, F. Winner, J. Dragesco; 24, R. König; 25, J. P. Champroux, J. P. Varin, P. Summ; 26, P. Nief; 27, J. P. Varin; 28-29, J. C. Maes, M. Colas, C. M. Moiton, S. Cordier; 30, M. Colas; 31, S. Cordier, J. P. Heruy; 33, J. P. Varin, J. M. Labat, Frédéric; 35, J. M. Labat; 37, J. L. Le Moigne, J. P. Varin; 39, J. P. Varin, Axel; 41, T. Walker, H. Engels; 43, J. P. Jaubert, J. M. Labat; 44, J. P. Jaubert; 45, F. Gohier, T. Dressler

Printed in the United States of America

1 2 3 4 5 6 7 8 9 02 01 00 99 98

CONTENTS

THE NEED FOR SHELTER

Most animals need to protect themselves and their young from different kinds of dangers.

Safety from hunters

Any animal can become the prey of a predator from another species that hunts it for food. To keep safe, an animal must be able to camouflage or hide itself and, if possible, avoid being caught.

Guarding their young

The fragile young of many species are unable to survive if they are left on their own shortly after birth. This is especially true for mammals and most birds, which keep their young near them to protect and feed them.

Left: **This owl's nest is safely hidden in a hole in a tree trunk.**

Above: **A rabbit looks to see if it is safe to leave its burrow.**

Protection from cold

Some animals, such as cranes, ducks, and storks, migrate to spend winter in warmer regions. Other animals stay in the same area and must protect themselves from the cold in various ways throughout the winter. Some find a hiding place and sleep during these months. This is called hibernation.

Right: **These baby magpies wait in the safety of the nest for their parents to return with food.**

5

PROTECTION AND CAMOUFLAGE

Above: **These fish are protected by their color, which blends in with the water and provides camouflage.**

Many animals can find shelter among the plants in their natural habitat.

In the forest, moose and deer take refuge among trees and foliage. On the African savanna, only the surrounding plants protect large mammals.

Many fish swim freely among the algae and other aquatic plants. These great swimmers, such as the tuna, do not shelter themselves.

Camouflage protection

Animals are effectively protected if their color and shape keep other animals from seeing them in their surroundings. Many animals have spotted or striped fur or skin. This helps them blend in with lights and shadows of the

surrounding plants. Some animals, such as the spider crab, grow fibers over their bodies. Others cover themselves with plant or mineral debris from their environment.

Most fish have a dark color on the top section of their bodies. When viewed from above, these fish blend in with the bottom of the body of water. In contrast, their bellies are light colored and hard to see in the light on the surface of the water if a predator looks up from below.

Many flat fish can change the color of the side facing up, depending on which direction they are facing.

Above: **Deer take shelter among the trees.**

Right: **The caddis fly larva, which lives in running water, uses silk to bind pebbles, twigs, and shells into a case that protects and hides it.**

The Shell: Natural Protection

The bivalve mollusks, such as mussels, oysters, and clams, have shells divided into two parts. Other mollusks have only one shell. It may be plain, like the limpet's, which is shaped like a cone. It might also be spiraled, like the periwinkle's. Single-shelled mollusks are called gastropods.

Mollusk shells increase in size gradually, along with the growth of the rest of their bodies. Shells show growth rings.

Mollusks

Most mollusks secrete a chalky shell material from their bodies, which surrounds and protects them. Other mollusks, such as slugs and octopuses, do not have shells.

The cuttlefish's shell is a calcium-containing plate embedded in its body. These "cuttlefish bones" often wash up on beaches.

Corals

Corals are tiny, soft-bodied animals that live in colonies of thousands of individuals. Each secretes a hard substance into a cuplike shape that joins them to the others and protects them. In time, these huge colonies form great masses called reefs. Fish with pointed jaws graze among the corals, searching for food.

MOLTING TO CHANGE SHELLS

Crustacean shells

A crustacean's body, as with shrimp, crayfish, and crabs, is protected by a jointed shell.

Since the shell cannot grow while the crustacean grows, it must shed its shell several times. This is called molting.

In molting, the shell splits across the back and the animal crawls out. During the dangerous time that the animal's new shell is soft, the animal absorbs water and swells to a larger size.

It usually hides for as long as it takes for the new shell to harden and protect it.

The hermit crab

The hermit crab is a small crustacean with an armored head and claws, but a soft abdomen.

To protect itself, the animal finds an empty shell, usually from a snail. It backs into the shell so only the front of its body sticks out.

When the hermit crab grows too large for its shell, it finds a larger one in which to live.

For added protection, the hermit crab may also "plant" a sea anemone on the top of its shelter.

Right: **Living lobsters are blue or green. Cooking turns them red.**

Left: **This beetle sometimes is called a rhinoceros beetle because of its horn.**

Opposite, bottom: **The hermit crab hides its soft abdomen in an empty shell.**

Insects with shells

All insects have outer coverings that vary in hardness and thickness. Members of the beetle family have hard, shell-like covers. When resting, rigid elytra protect their wings. Insects also molt several times as they grow. They lose their old covering each time.

In metamorphic, or shape-changing, insects, such as butterflies and bees, only the larvae molt. The adults remain at the same size.

Right: **The porcupine protects itself with quills.**

Right: **An armadillo, like this one from Chile, can roll quickly into a ball to protect itself from predators.**

Right: **A coat of hornlike scales protects this pangolin, or scaly anteater. It lives in tropical Africa and Asia.**

ARMORED VERTEBRATES

Well-protected reptiles

The tortoise has a spinal column; it is a vertebrate. It also has a hard, horny shell. Its head, legs, tail, and reproductive organs are outside the shell. In times of danger, many tortoises retreat entirely into their shells.

Crocodiles do not have rigid shells. They are protected by hard scales reinforced by bony plates.

Mammals with armor

The pangolin's body is covered with large, hard scales that make it resemble a pine cone. It climbs trees and eats insects.

When threatened, the pangolin rolls itself into a ball to protect its soft underside.

Armadillos are protected by jointed armor with three, six, or nine bands. They live in the Americas, where they dig in the ground for food.

Hedgehogs and porcupines have prickly quills that bristle when the animals feel threatened.

The spiny anteater of Australia also has sharp quills for protection.

Below: **This giant tortoise lives in the Galápagos Islands.**

SHELLS ARE NOT PERFECT PROTECTION

Limited protection

It may seem that the best shelter for an animal is an outside covering for its body. However, even animals with protected bodies can fall prey to predators. For example, the parrotfish grazes on corals with its strong, beaklike mouth.

Mollusk shells cannot provide protection against the beaks of certain birds. Starfish can force open mollusk shells.

Many mollusks and crustaceans bury themselves in sand or seek shelter in rock crevices. But birds with long beaks still can dislodge and eat them. Each species of invertebrate buries itself in sand or mud at the same depth. Birds eat different prey according to the length of their beaks.

No guarantees

Ever since life appeared on Earth, some species have become extinct even with shells. Other species with less protection have continued to develop. Many armored water animals have been found only as fossils, having become extinct millions of years ago.

The squid, related to the octopus, has no outside shell, and after millions of years remains unchanged.

Below: **This hard shell cannot provide protection against a starfish.**

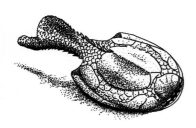

Above: **This armored fish, now extinct, was discovered as a fossil.**

Right: **The squid is a mollusk with no outside shell. This characteristic has not changed for millions of years.**

Below: **On a beach at low tide, curlews and godwits search for invertebrate prey.**

INSECTS PROTECT THEMSELVES

Protection for pupas

Many insects hatch as larva, often looking very different from the adults. They must metamorphose, or change shape.

Caterpillars go through metamorphosis to turn into butterflies or moths.

Sometimes, the stages of metamorphosis require a period of inactivity. The larva generally secretes material to create a rigid envelope to protect itself, mainly from drying out. The butterfly larva's protective case is called a chrysalis. The larva inside is pupating.

Some moth caterpillars weave a protective cocoon around themselves with silk thread they secrete from special glands called spinnerets. Then they safely pupate inside.

A silky nest

In European pine and oak forests, long rows of caterpillars sometimes line up to eat the leaves or needles of trees.

Then, following a trail of silken thread they have unwound, they return together to their nest, a ball of silky material they have constructed.

These are processionary caterpillars, which live together. Later, after metamorphosing into moths, they abandon the nest and scatter.

Right: **A butterfly caterpillar develops a chrysalis to protect itself during pupation.**

The cricket's burrow

We can hear the cricket singing but seldom see it. This is because it sends its song out from a tiny burrow in the ground.

Scratching gently at the entrance of the cricket's burrow usually will make the curious insect peek out to investigate.

Left: **A male cricket guards the entrance to its burrow.**

Above: **Processionary caterpillars in a pine forest return to their nest.**

Left: **The adult swallowtail butterfly leaves its chrysalis at the end of its metamorphosis.**

DWELLINGS OF COLONIAL INSECTS

Above: **All the wasps in this nest are from eggs laid by the queen.**

Nests of paper

In spring, each female wasp and hornet finds a hole in the ground or in a tree where she will start a colony. There she builds a nest out of paper she makes by chewing wood. She lays several eggs, each in its own six-sided cell. In about two weeks, the first wasps hatch. These wasps increase the nest's basic population and will then hunt for caterpillars and flies to feed the next batches of larvae.

Potter wasps build nests from clay. They are much smaller than paper nests.

The wax beehive

Bees usually construct their hives in the wild; for example, in a hollow tree. In hives constructed for bees by humans, the bees organize themselves in the same way and live in large colonies.

The queen bee, the largest bee in the hive, is

the only female able to lay eggs. The worker bees take care of the eggs she places in the honeycombs. They also feed the larvae.

The worker bees build the honeycombs, ventilate the hive by beating their wings, and carefully guard the entrance to the hive. They also forage among flowers for the pollen and nectar needed in the hive and turn the nectar into honey. Male bees, called drones, do no work.

Above: **The queen bee lays an egg in each cell. Workers cap the cells with wax until the larvae hatch.**

Below: **After metamorphosis, a new adult worker bee leaves its cell.**

A City
Under Ground:
The Anthill

The ground in a pine forest sometimes contains a dome made of twigs and pine needles. This is an anthill, which shelters from 100,000 to 500,000 red ants.

Some kinds of ants live in rotted wood or old trees. Other ant species take shelter entirely under ground, and only their energetic activity reveals the entrance.

The ant workers' most important task is to feed and protect the young ants in the hive.

Reproduction is carried out by several females, also called queens. After mating with a male, they lose their wings and spend the rest of their lives,

Above: **Weaver ants assemble the leaves they will join with the silky threads secreted by their larvae.**

Left: **A dome-shaped anthill made by red ants.**

Sewing nests

Some ants, called weaver ants, make their nests by sewing leaves together.

While a few workers hold the leaves in place, other workers bring the larvae, which secrete silky threads.

Holding the larvae in their jaws, the ants weave them back and forth to fasten the edges together with silk.

Above: **If an anthill is damaged, the ants' first task is to save the larvae in their cocoons.**

which can be five to ten years, laying thousands of eggs underground.

Busy ant workers

Worker ants carry the eggs to the chambers and keep them at even temperatures. The workers also regurgitate food to feed the larvae and tear open the cocoons as the larvae reach adulthood. Other workers guard the entrance. They recognize the scents of their own ants and reject those that do not belong.

Worker ants also supply grain, insects, and aphids. They feed on honeydew, a sweet juice aphids excrete.

TERMITES: BUILDERS AND FARMERS

Tropical termites

In the African savanna stand large clay mounds several feet (m) high and hard as cement. These are truly skyscrapers to the tiny insects that built them — termites.

Termite mounds can be 16-20 feet (5-6 m) tall and as much as 98 feet (30 m) wide at the base.

Termite mounds act as chimneys that ventilate the

Above: **Tiny insects built this African termite mound almost as tall as a tree.**

huge nest, carrying away hot air. Inside, a large cavern several feet (m) wide shelters many small chambers and tunnels.

One termite mound can house the king and queen termites (responsible for reproduction), about 500,000 workers, and 350,000 soldiers in charge of defending the mound.

Besides these, there are about 150,000 young, winged males and females. When these termites leave the nest, they will form

new reproductive couples that will then build new termite mounds. However, many predators wait outside the termite mound for them to emerge, so only a few young termites that leave their home nest actually survive.

Along with their abilities as builders, termites have good farming skills. They often grow fungi under-

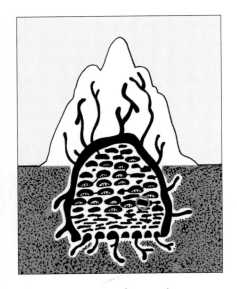

Above: **Cutaway of a termite mound. The chamber where the queen lays her eggs is circled. The white masses in some chambers are fungi.**

ground. Fungi help them digest their food, which is mostly wood.

Termite invaders

In North America, not all termites build mounds. Some attack the wood in people's houses and cause a lot of damage. This destruction usually is not noticed until it becomes a serious problem.

Left: **A soldier termite in a chamber where fungi grow.**

Below: **Workers surrounding the large, white queen termite feed her and carry away the eggs she lays.**

BUILDING FOR OTHER PURPOSES

Spinning a trap

Garden spiders spin their webs in lovely geometric designs. To weave these elaborate webs, they use strands of silk that they secrete from special glands in their abdomen called spinnerets.

The young spider knows instinctively how to spin a web. Each species of spider makes webs in the same design. The spider strings a frame of dry threads firmly between plants. Then it weaves strands across the web, going through the center. Finally, it traces a tight, sticky spiral, solidly glued to each strand.

This transparent web is now ready to trap insects unlucky enough to touch the web and become stuck. The spider often stays in the center of the web. If it leaves the web, it keeps a thread tied to the center as an alarm, so it can return immediately

Above: **This spider waits for an insect to come into its web.**

Right: **The trapdoor spider under the lid of its underground home.**

24

if prey becomes trapped. The spider spins silk around its prey, covers it with digestive fluid to dissolve it, then drinks the liquid meal and discards the rest.

Some species of spiders spin webs in other shapes, such as a funnel. Trap-door spiders dig holes in the ground for shelter.

Tunnels to go

Many animals dig holes in the ground or in trees. They live under ground or in the tree holes and must go out for food.

Not all animals dig for shelter. The earthworm finds food in the ground and then excretes the waste at the surface. Some termites live inside trees, tunneling through the wood.

Underwater air

To dive under water, the water spider makes a silken bell, which fills with air as it moves farther down into the water. This delicate structure allows the water spider to spend long periods of time under water.

Above: Termite larvae have eaten their way through the tree, leaving paths behind.

Above: The water spider dives under water, breathing with a silken bell filled with air.

Nests to Hold Bird Eggs

To hatch, a bird's eggs must be kept warm, or incubated. The parent bird(s) often sit on the eggs to incubate them.

Some baby birds, such as chickens, partridges, and ostriches, can walk and find food as soon as they hatch. Young ducks hatch knowing how to swim. These baby birds can leave the nest almost right away and follow their mother eagerly to the nearest pond to swim.

The nests of these birds are usually simple, often just a hole in the ground padded with a little dry grass. The partridge, quail, and lark make this kind of nest.

The baby birds in most other species have no feathers and cannot leave the nest or feed themselves. They stay in the nest, fed by their parents, until they grow feathers and become strong enough to fly. These birds build strong nests to help protect the young from predators.

Nest building

Before laying eggs, birds build a nest. Every bird of the same species builds the same kind of nest by instinct. Other animals have instincts, too. They can locate food and shelter and can reproduce and raise their young by instinct, without being taught by any others.

Opposite: **A mallard duck with her ducklings.**

Left: **With their beaks wide open, these baby blue tits wait to be fed.**

A Nest
for Each
Bird

Right: The raven rears young in a nest of twigs perched high off the ground.

Above: This grebe, a swamp bird, sits on a floating nest, which is a raft made of reeds. Coots and sometimes water hens also nest this way.

Right: The woodpecker builds a nest in a tree trunk.

Above, left: **Fish bones litter this kingfisher's riverbank nest.**

Above, right: **This red warbler's nest is located in the reeds of a swamp.**

Below: **A swallow's nest is built of mud.**

Unusual Nests

Many small birds weave their nests from long, thin materials, such as grass. The warbler builds its nest out of leaves. It sews them together with plant fibers it holds in its beak.

One roof for many

In Africa, some weaver birds build their nests side by side under a common roof that shelters them all.

Decorating nests

Some birds in Australia and the South Pacific have unusual mating customs.

The male bowerbird uses twigs to build a structure called a bower (named after a lady's room in medieval times), which is different for each species. He decorates it with wild berries, shells, and colored stones.

When a female is attracted by this decorative structure and enters it, the male offers her a gift of fruit, stones, or a shell, and then mates with her. They build a new, plain nest together for raising their brood.

The satin bowerbird and the regent bowerbird decorate their bowers with strips of bark and a paint made from saliva mixed with charcoal, fruit pulp, and wood pulp.

Borrowed nests

The cuckoo does not build its own nest. The female lays each of her eggs in the nests of other bird species. After waiting for the owners to leave the nest, she quickly takes one of their eggs out of the nest and leaves one of her own in its place.

Left: **This bowerbird waits to offer a gift to the female attracted by the setting he built and decorated.**

The nest's occupants do not notice anything, although the baby cuckoo often hatches first. Since the baby cuckoo does not like sharing the nest with the other eggs, it often pushes them out of the nest and becomes the only surviving baby in that nest.

The adult birds become its adoptive parents. They are not bothered by the wide-open mouth of their hungry baby. They bring it insects and worms until it leaves the nest for good.

An adult female cuckoo often lays her eggs in the nests of the same species of birds that raised her.

Right: **The well-fed baby cuckoo grows bigger than its foster parents (here, red warblers).**

Right: **Weaver birds in Africa build their hanging nests under the same large roof.**

OTHER
NEST-BUILDERS

Above: **The male stickleback watches its nest.**

Many nests

The eagle stays only in a large area where it keeps several nests in high, hard-to-reach places, often on steep cliffs. It lives in each of the nests at different times. These nests usually are made of branches and brushwood.

Rare fish nests

Most fish lay thousands of eggs in the water, but only a small number of them will reach adulthood because predators eat most of them. Some species protect their eggs by laying them in the mud or in a rock crevice.

The male stickleback, a tiny river fish, builds a silky nest out of grass, where it invites female fish to lay eggs. Then the male guards the eggs in the nest until they hatch.

The male Siamese fighting fish builds a floating nest made of air bubbles trapped in its sticky saliva to hold its eggs. It stays near to guard the eggs and the young.

Other animal nests

The squirrel builds a nest in a tree to raise its young and protect itself in the cold season. The garden dormouse sometimes lives in a bird's nest.

A female crocodile lays eggs in a hole she digs in the ground. She watches the eggs and protects the young until they can care for themselves.

A female python digs a hole and incubates her eggs by coiling herself up around them.

Right: **This squirrel spends the winter in a hollow tree.**

Below: **A female crocodile watches one of her young.**

REFUGE FOR THE WINTER

Hibernation

Some mammals spend the winter months in a state of deep sleep, called hibernation. They must search for a shelter in which to stay.

If a brown bear cannot find a cave or some other shelter to use, it will burrow in among the roots of a large tree.

The marmot, which lives in a shallow hole during the summer, digs a deep burrow in the prairie. Twelve or fifteen marmots will hibernate together.

The bat hangs upside-down in a cave. Like the marmot, the bat's body temperature drops to match the air temperature, so it must be careful to avoid freezing.

Voles do not hibernate, but they spend the winter in deep holes that keep out snow and cold.

Left: **Sheltered in a cave, bats can sleep all winter.**

Other winter shelters

Some animals have only the forest for shelter. Others find various protected places.

Deer gather in an area with thick foliage for the cold winter. This is called yarding up. The deer return to this spot for rest and protection.

In a climate with mild winters, the wild boar lives in a thicket — a dense growth of shrubs or small trees. It also likes to be near a mudhole so it can wallow.

A rabbit also lives in a thicket and often makes a trail to it, which hunters have learned to recognize.

Above: **A bear enters the shelter that will protect it all winter.**

MAMMAL BURROWS

Below: **At the entrance to its home, a rabbit guards its young.**

Many desert animals spend the days in burrows to avoid the intense heat. They come out only at night. In more temperate climates, the opposite is often true — the animals come out by day and stay inside their burrows at night as protection against the cold.

Life underground

The mole spends its life under ground. It is nearly blind — its tiny eyes can only distinguish day from night. Its front feet are like shovels that it uses to dig burrows. The soil thrown out while digging forms a mound, called a molehill. Inside lies a

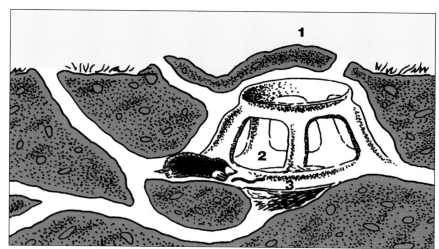

large room with tunnels that lead to other rooms. A pantry stores earthworms and insects the mole has found while digging. Passages to the outside provide ventilation.

Rabbit burrows

Rabbits live together in burrows that have several openings to the outside. A female will move to her own little room to give birth to four or five baby rabbits. She nurses them for about three weeks.

When she leaves this chamber to get food, she blocks the entrance against predators, such as skunks, weasels, and ferrets.

Top: **Cutaway view of a molehill: 1. Molehill 2. Chamber 3. Nest**

Above: **The mole sticks its nose out of its burrow.**

NEIGHBORS, BUT DIFFERENT

Badger burrows

Badgers live in groups and dig burrows with several exits. The burrows have chambers lined with dry grass and straw. In the largest chamber, the female gives birth to three to five babies. She nurses them every night for a month. Burrows are kept very clean, and any litter is thrown out.

Badgers allow foxes to live near them, even though foxes do not have clean habits.

Left: **The badger sticks its snout out of its burrow.**

Right: **Cutaway view of a badger burrow:**
1. Chamber (room)
2. Nursery
3, 4. Exits
5. Mound
6. Chamber

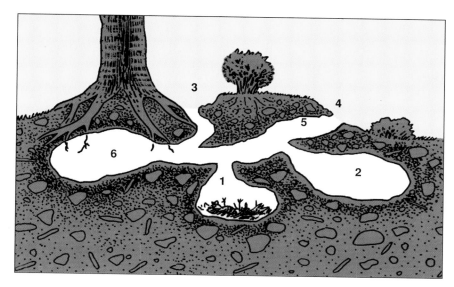

Left: Cutaway view
of a fox burrow:
1. Pantry
2. Playroom
3, 4. Exits
5. Covered entrance
6. Family room

Smelly foxhole

Foxes often take over burrows abandoned by other animals. However, no animal would want to take over a fox's hole — it smells too bad.

Besides the large family room and the playroom for the fox cubs, the fox usually will dig a room or pit to use for storing the game birds it eats. The dead birds do not stay fresh long and soon begin to smell. Most rooms in a foxhole have separate paths to the outside.

Right: **Baby foxes explore the tunnels of their burrow.**

BUILDING LODGES AND DAMS

Above: **Canadian beavers have built a dam and made an artificial pond. The lodge is the mound behind the dam.**

Opposite: **A beaver at work on the top of its lodge.**

Beavers live mainly on riverbanks. Two beavers can actually create a pond on a river by blocking the water with a dam built from tree trunks, stones, and branches.

When the water stops rising, the beavers build a lodge about 16 feet (5 m) wide and 5 feet (1.5 m) high. Covered in mud, the lodge looks like a mound with no openings.

There are usually two rooms inside the lodge, with openings into the water. A ventilation shaft brings in fresh air.

Beavers stay busy gathering building materials and working to keep the dam and lodge in good repair.

Some beavers dig dens in the riverbank when the water's current is too strong for a dam. The den's large central room is above the water level. A special shaft provides ventilation. The den also has an entrance tunnel under the water.

Winter stockpile

Beavers collect branches to store under the water for food during winter when ice covers the pond.

Wild hamsters hoard food supplies inside their burrows for use in winter.

Field mice also store grains and tubers. Sometimes, field mice will find shelter in a stable or a grain silo and take food from humans, although this can be risky!

PROTECTED BY HUMANS

Domestic animals

Through the centuries, humans have acquired animals to provide milk, meat, leather, and eggs, and to help with work. These wild animals were captured and tamed.

Dogs were the first animals to be domesticated and kept by humans — about twelve thousand years ago. Then followed, in order, sheep, goats, pigs, and cows. About nine thousand years ago humans captured and tamed Asian elephants, camels, horses, and donkeys. Five thousand years ago came chickens, geese, cats, and rabbits.

Humans bred these animals with their most useful qualities in mind; for example, higher milk-producing cows, faster horses, and heavier chickens. In this way, these animals changed from

Above: **Raised in batteries, these chickens can only eat and lay eggs.**

their wild ancestors. It is easy, for example, to see the difference between the wild boar and today's farmyard pig.

With these changing conditions, domesticated animals became less able to fend for themselves. That is why humans now must provide food and shelter for these animals.

Left: **On a farm, cows are sheltered in barns.**

Animals in zoos

For many, many years, people lived in nature. As cities developed, people saw fewer animals, and their curiosity toward exotic, unusual animals grew. In the 1800s, people who no longer lived near nature wanted to see the animal world, so zoos were created in the larger cities. There, visitors could see up-close animals that came from faraway countries. Most often, they were in cages.

Later, many zoos began to construct artificial environments that more closely resembled the animals' natural habitats. This practice eliminated the need for cages and gave the animals more space and freedom to move.

In some zoos, visitors can drive around vast enclosed areas and see the animals. It has become possible to observe many animals as if they are in their natural habitats.

Below: **The polar bears in this zoo live in an artificial arctic environment.**

PROTECTING ANIMALS
IN FREEDOM

Right: **In California, this desert area is now a national park.**

Natural parks

To protect endangered species, large areas of land have been set aside by governments as nature preserves, where public access is controlled. In these areas, visitors can observe animals living their lives naturally.

The oldest natural park is Yellowstone National Park, created in 1872 in the United States, mainly in the Rocky Mountains of Montana.

Banff National Park, the oldest park in Canada, was established in 1885.

Australia saw its first park in 1879, and New Zealand established its first in 1894.

South Africa's Kruger National Park was formed in 1898. Most of Africa's parks were established about fifty years ago.

Above: **Yellowstone National Park was the first established natural park.**

Top: **Ecrins National Park in the French Alps.**

Left: **One of the largest natural parks in Africa is in Kenya.**

GLOSSARY

adapt — to change behavior or adjust needs in order to survive in changing conditions.

algae — water plants with no roots, stems, or leaves.

bivalve — a shell divided into two; bivalve mollusks include mussels and clams.

chrysalis — a butterfly pupa's protective covering.

cocoon — the protective case of the pupa of many insects. Moths spin cocoons of silk.

colony — a community where all members live and work together.

crevice — a narrow opening in rock, such as a crack or split.

crustaceans — animals with a hard, jointed outer shell that live mostly in water. Lobsters, crabs, and shrimp are crustaceans.

debris — scattered remains.

environment — the surroundings in which plants and animals live.

excrete — to get rid of waste from an animal's body.

fossils — the remains of plants or animals from an earlier time period that are found in rock or in Earth's crust.

fungus (*pl* **fungi**) — a primitive plant that cannot make its own food and must live on food made by other organisms, living or dead.

geometric — formed from regular straight lines, circles, curves, or squares.

habitat — the natural home of a plant or animal.

hibernation — a state of rest or inactivity in which most bodily functions, such as heartbeat and breathing, slow down.

instinct — a behavior pattern that is inborn, not learned.

invertebrates — animals that do not have a backbone.

larva (*pl* **larvae**) — the wingless, wormlike form of a newly hatched insect; the stage after the egg but before full development.

metamorphosis — a complete change in form or appearance; in most insects, this change occurs in stages: egg, larva, pupa, and adult.

migrate — to move from one place or climate to another, usually on a seasonal basis.

mollusks — animals with a hard, outer shell, usually living in water, such as clams and snails.

nectar — a sweet liquid found in many flowers, often used as a food source by insects.

nourishment — any substance that helps an animal grow, develop, and survive; food.

nurse — to drink milk from the mother's body.

predators — animals that hunt and eat other animals.

prey — animals hunted and eaten by other animals.

pupa — the third stage in the life-cycle of most insects, between larva and adult.

refuge — a place of safety.

savanna — a flat landscape, usually covered with coarse grasses and scattered trees.

secrete — to give off a substance, usually liquid.

species — animals or plants that are closely related and often similar in behavior and appearance. Members of the same species are capable of breeding together.

temperate climate — the climate zones lying between the tropics and the polar regions, with warm summers and cold winters.

tuber — a swelling in the root system of some plants, where food is stored.

BOOKS TO READ

Animal Architects. Donald J. Crump
(National Geographic)

Animal Defenses. Jeremy Cherfas
(Lerner Group)

Animal Magic for Kids series. (Gareth Stevens)

Crustaceans: Armored Omnivores. Secrets of the Animal World series. Andreu Llamas
(Gareth Stevens)

Endangered Animals! ENDANGERED! series.
Bob Burton (Gareth Stevens)

Exploring Fresh Water Habitats.
Diane Snowball (Mondo Publishing)

Fish. Wonderful World of Animals series.
Beatrice MacLeod (Gareth Stevens)

Hiding Out: Camouflage in the Wild. James
Martin (Crown Books for Young Readers)

In Peril series. Barbara J. Behm and
Jean-Christophe Balouet (Gareth Stevens)

Mistaken Identity. Joyce Pope
(Raintree Steck-Vaughn)

The New Creepy Crawly Collection series.
(Gareth Stevens)

Why Are Animals Endangered? Isaac Asimov
(Gareth Stevens)

Why Are Whales Vanishing? Isaac Asimov
(Gareth Stevens)

Wings Along the Waterway. Mary B. Brown
(Orchard Books)

VIDEOS

Animal Architecture.
(Phoenix/BFA Films & Video)

Animal Defenses.
(Agency for Instructional Technology)

Animal Habitats (rev.).
(Phoenix/BFA Films & Video)

The Bird's Nest.
(Coronet, The Multimedia Company)

How Nature Protects Animals.
(Encyclopædia Britannica Educational
Corporation)

WEB SITES

http://magicnet.net/~mgodwin/

www.isle-of-man.com/interests/shark/
scient.htm

www.teelfamily.com/activities/polarbear/

www.5tigers.org/cubs.htm

INDEX